Sweet Delights

Sweet Delights

Delectable ideas for mouthwatering
desserts and tempting treats

Emma Summer

LORENZ BOOKS

First published in 1999 by
Lorenz Books

© 1999 Anness Publishing Limited

Lorenz Books
is an imprint of
Anness Publishing Inc.
27 West 20th Street
New York, NY 10011 (800) 354-9657

ISBN 0 7548 0274 4

Publisher: Joanna Lorenz
Executive Editor: Linda Fraser
Project Editors: Sarah Ainley, Emma Brown and Emma Clegg
Designers: Patrick McLeavey & Partners
Illustrator: Anna Koska
Photographers: Karl Adamson, Edward Allwright, Steve
Baxter, James Duncan, Michelle Garrett, Amanda Heywood,
Don Last and Thomas Odulate
Recipes: Carla Capalbo, Jacqueline Clark, Carole Clements,
Joanna Farrow, Rafi Fernandez, Christine France,
Sarah Gates, Shirley Gill, Ruby Le Bois, Laura Washburn,
Stephen Wheeler and Elizabeth Wolf-Cohen
Reader: Diane Ashmore
Production Controller: Ben Worley

Previously published in two separate volumes *The Little Dessert Cookbook*
and *The Little Ice Cream Cookbook*.

Printed and bound in Singapore

10 9 8 7 6 5 4 3 2 1

Contents

Introduction

The strong-willed reach resolutely for the fruit bowl at the conclusion of every meal, but most of us would much rather be treated to a luxurious, magical, spirit-lifting dessert. Cool and creamy, sweet and fruity, or simply drowning in chocolate, desserts are destined to remain on the menu. Whatever the season, there's a perfect sweet delight waiting in the wings, whether it be a comforting Blackberry Cobbler to chase away autumn blues, a Watermelon Sorbet to celebrate a lazy summer's day or a Chocolate Pavlova with Chocolate Curls to bring your dinner party to a memorable finale.

When planning a menu, choose a dessert to complement the preceding courses. A hearty casserole calls for a simple sorbet or fruit salad, whereas a plainly grilled fish dish could precede something rich and creamy,

such as an Amaretto Soufflé or a Minted Raspberry Bavarois. If you plan to spoil your guests with a self-indulgent masterpiece such as Hazelnut Meringue Torte with Pears, then keep the rest of the meal as low-key as possible.

When serving eight or more, it is a good idea to offer a choice of desserts. These should contrast in color and content, so perhaps offer a fruit-filled Autumn Pudding alongside a Chocolate Cake with Coffee Sauce. Where appropriate, offer a choice of accompaniments, such as plain yogurt and whipped cream. Fresh fruit is always a favorite, and there are plenty of ideas here for both hot and cold desserts. One simple idea for serving fruit used in Thai cooking is to cut fresh pineapple, melon and papaya into similar-sized wedges and overlap them on a decorative platter with orange and pink grapefruit segments around the rim.

Ice cream desserts can be as simple or as elaborate as desired. Making your own ice cream also means that you control the ingredients as well as the cost. Yogurt, buttermilk or fromage frais will make lower-calorie versions, liqueurs can be added to please dinner party guests and fruit purées can be transformed into luscious sorbets. After a rich meal, serve a simple ice or a granita. Parties call for sumptuous parfaits—ice cream or whipped cream layered in a tall glass with chocolate or fruit, and then frozen—or sundaes that are assembled at the last minute.

Decorating desserts can be a creative exercise. The most ordinary mousse surrounded by a fresh fruit coulis feathered with

cream looks exquisite, while rosettes of cream spiked with chocolate leaves would make the perfect topping for a rich mocha mousse. Another idea is to use the main ingredient in the dessert, decorating a strawberry cheesecake with chocolate-tipped strawberries for example, or Oranges in Caramel Sauce with strips of blanched orange peel.

This recipe collection ranges from fruit desserts to classic custards, and also includes classic favorites such as Fruit-filled Bread Pudding, Baked Caramel Custard and Cherry Pudding. Coffee and chocolate desserts get a chapter to themselves, and with recipes such as Coffee Gelatin with Amaretti Cream and Chocolate Cream Puffs included, you may be sure everyone will get more than their just desserts!

7

Ingredients

BUTTER
Use unsalted butter for desserts. Store it in the refrigerator, in the original wrapper. Freeze unopened sticks in a plastic freezer bag for up to six months.

CHOCOLATE
Most supermarkets stock a good range of semi-sweet, milk and white chocolate and chocolate products, including sprinkles, chips and buttons. For the best results in cooking, use chocolate with a cocoa solid content of at least 50 percent. Chocolate with a high cocoa butter content melts easily. Unsweetened cocoa powder is used in baking.

COFFEE
Coffee adds a rich, unmistakable flavor to cakes, desserts and ice cream. It is used in instant powder or crushed granular form for cakes and cookies. For a rich dessert, use a coffee liqueur such as Tia Maria for flavoring and decorate the dessert with coffee beans dipped in chocolate.

CREAM
Light cream has 18 percent butterfat and is mainly used for pouring. In whipping cream the butterfat content increases to 35–38 percent. When whipped, the cream will hold its shape briefly, but for a dessert decoration, use heavy cream (48 percent butterfat). Crème fraîche is a thick, sour cream made from light cream, but with less fat.

EGGS
Unless recipes specify otherwise, use medium-size eggs. Always buy eggs from a reputable supplier, preferably date-stamped, and use them fresh. This is especially important when the eggs in a recipe are not cooked.

SUGAR
The darker the sugar, the stronger the flavor of molasses you will taste. Useful choices for desserts are granulated sugar, superfine sugar and light and dark brown sugars. Confectioners' sugar is also useful for lightly sprinkling on finished desserts.

Fruits

CITRUS FRUITS

Lemons and limes are interchangeable in most recipes, but lime is more scented and has an intense flavor, so use it more sparingly. Oranges are available year-round and are a good choice for desserts—use the zest or juice, or cut the fruit into segments. Satsumas, tangerines, mandarins and clementines are small citrus fruits that are interchangeable in most recipes.

STONE FRUITS

Use apricots raw or lightly poached. Cherries should be firm and glossy. Plums are available in dessert and cooking varieties. They range in color from pale gold to black. For cooking, use slightly under-ripe plums. Choose white peaches for the sweetest flavor, and yellow for a more aromatic flavor.

9

BERRIES

Blackberries can be found growing wild or cultivated. Brambles are usually smaller than cultivated blackberries, with a stronger flavor. When they are not available, use raspberries or black currants. Black currants, red currants and white currants are occasionally available at farmers' markets and gourmet food stores. Raspberries, black raspberries and loganberries are all delicious, juicy berries. Strawberries are best eaten fresh and ripe; they tend to lose texture and color if frozen. Dessert gooseberries are sweet. Cooking varieties are smaller, firm, green and slightly sharp.

EXOTIC FRUITS

Figs are green-or purple-skinned fruit with sweet, pinkish-red flesh. Eat figs whole or peeled. Fresh dates are sweet and juicy, and are more succulent than dried dates. Kiwi fruit are available all year round. Peel them thinly and slice the bright-green flesh.

ORCHARD & VINE FRUITS

Apples and pears are versatile fruits; both dessert and culinary varieties can be cooked. Grapes are available in many varieties and vary in color from pale green to deep purple. The sweetness varies, so taste before you buy.

Simple Sauces

APRICOT

Heat ¾ cup apricot jam with ¼ cup water. Let boil for 10 minutes, stirring continuously, then press through a sieve into a heatproof bowl. Stir in lemon juice to taste, and add a little orange-flavored liqueur, if desired. Serve the sauce warm, poured over ice cream.

BUTTERSCOTCH

Melt ¼ cup butter with ½ cup brown sugar and 3 tablespoons corn syrup in a heavy saucepan over medium heat. Bring the mixture to a boil, stirring constantly, then cook over low heat until golden brown. Serve the sauce hot, over ice cream.

CHOCOLATE

Gently heat ⅔ cup heavy cream with ¼ cup diced butter and ¼ cup sugar in a large saucepan, stirring until smooth. Let cool, then stir in 1 cup chocolate chips or semi-sweet chocolate, broken into chunks, until melted, and serve hot.

LEMON & LIME

Peel the zest from one lemon and two limes and squeeze the juice from the fruit. Place the zest in a saucepan, cover with water and bring to a boil. Drain through a sieve and reserve the zest. Mix ¼ cup sugar in a bowl with 1½ tablespoons arrowroot, and add a little water to give a smooth paste. Heat ¾ cup of water, pour in the arrowroot, and stir until the sauce boils and thickens. Stir in 1 tablespoon sugar, the citrus juice and reserved zest, and serve hot. Sprinkle the dessert with fresh mint to decorate.

FRUIT COULIS

Wash and hull 3 cups of raspberries, strawberries or blackberries and drain them on paper towels. Purée the berries in a blender or food processor. Turn the machine on and off a few times and scrape down the bowl to be sure all the berries are evenly puréed. For soft berries with small seeds, press the purée through a fine-mesh nylon sieve. Add 3–6 tablespoons of sifted confectioners' sugar to taste and a litttle lemon juice and/or 1–2 tablespoons of liqueur. Stir well to dissolve the sugar completely.

Decorations

ALMONDS

Sliced or chopped, plain or toasted, almonds look good on creamy desserts. To toast them, spread sliced almonds in a single layer in a broiler pan and broil under medium heat until golden brown. Shake the pan often and check the nuts frequently, as they burn very easily. Press them onto the sides of a cold soufflé.

CHOCOLATE CARAQUE

Pour melted chocolate onto a clean, smooth surface, such as a marble slab. When set, draw a broad-bladed cook's knife lightly across the chocolate at an angle of 45 degrees, to cut thin layers that curl into scrolls. Alternatively, use a potato peeler on a bar of chocolate.

PIPED CHOCOLATE

Pipe melted chocolate designs on nonstick baking parchment. Spider webs, hearts and stars all look good, but lift them very carefully when transferring them to a cake or other dessert.

CHOCOLATE LEAVES

Select clean, unblemished, nonpoisonous leaves (rose leaves work well) and brush the undersides evenly with melted chocolate. Let set on nonstick baking parchment, then carefully peel off the chocolate leaves from the green leaves.

CONFECTIONERS' SUGAR/COCOA POWDER

Lay strips of paper or an old-fashioned paper doily over a dessert before dusting it with confectioners' sugar and/or cocoa powder. Carefully remove the paper to give a striped effect.

WHIPPED CREAM

Swirls, shells and rosettes of whipped cream are easy to achieve. Use a piping bag fitted with a large, star-shaped nozzle and keep the pressure even. Try not to over-handle cream. Take care not to overwhip cream for piping, as the cream will thicken further as it is forced out of the piping bag.

FROSTED FRUIT

For frosting fruit, have ready tiny bunches of grapes or black currants, or stemmed cherries. Brush the fruits with water, then roll or dip them into superfine sugar to coat. Let dry before using as a decoration. Unfrosted berries also make perfect decorations.

CITRUS ZEST

Top citrus sorbets with thinly pared orange, lemon or lime zest. Blanch the zest in boiling water, then drain and dry it thoroughly before use. Be sure to avoid the bitter white pith below the zest when preparing the fruit zest.

Techniques

WHISKING EGG WHITES

Separate the eggs carefully, by tapping the egg sharply against the edge of a mixing bowl. Hold the egg over the bowl and pull the two halves of the shell apart. Gently pass the yolk from one half to the other, letting the white run into the bowl. Place the egg whites in a clean, greasefree mixing bowl. Use a balloon whisk in a wide bowl for the greatest volume, although an electric hand beater will also do an efficient job. Whisk the whites until they are firm enough to hold either soft or stiff peaks when you lift the whisk, according to the recipe's specifications. Use the mixture immediately.

MELTING CHOCOLATE

The best way to melt chocolate is over very hot but not boiling water. Break the chocolate into a heat-proof bowl. Bring a saucepan of water to a boil, turn off the heat and set the bowl on top. Stir as the chocolate melts. Do not add any liquid to melting chocolate, and do not cover it during or after melting because any water or condensation could cause the chocolate to stiffen.

If you choose to melt chocolate in the microwave, check it at 5–10 second intervals, since it burns easily. Place in a microwave-safe bowl and heat on medium power for 2 minutes.

WHIPPING CREAM

Cooks with strong wrists swear that a rotary whisk gives the greatest volume, but a hand-held electric beater works well. Use heavy cream for decorating, and be careful not to overwhip the cream. It should just hold its shape and not look grainy.

MAKING CHOCOLATE CASES

Chocolate cases make perfect containers for mousses. Use a double layer of cupcake cases or candy cases. Using a brush or teaspoon, coat the inside of the inner case evenly with melted chocolate, invert, and let set. Peel off the paper and fill just before serving.

LINING A PASTRY PAN

A pastry shell that doesn't distort or shrink in baking is the desired result. The key to success is handling the dough gently.

Remove the chilled dough from the refrigerator and let it soften slightly at room temperature. Place it on a lightly floured surface. Flatten the dough into a neat round. Lightly flour the rolling pin. Roll out the dough working from the center to the edge and maintaining an even pressure. Lift and turn the dough occasionally to prevent it from sticking to the surface. Continue until the dough is 2 inches larger all around than the pan and about ⅛-inch thick. Set the rolling pin on the dough near one side. Fold the outside edge of the dough over the pin, then roll the rolling pin over the dough to wrap the dough around it. Gently unroll the dough over the pan, centring it as much as possible. With your fingertips, lift and ease the dough into the pan, gently pressing it into place.

PEELING, CORING & SLICING APPLES

Apples are very simple to prepare. Use a peeler to peel the fruit as thinly as possible, in a spiral movement, turning the fruit as you go.

Use a corer to press through the center of the apple and pull it out to remove the core. Alternately, cut the apple in quarters and cut out the core from each quarter with a knife.

Cut the apple in quarters and slice across each segment to make slices an even thickness. Sprinkle with lemon juice to prevent them from browning.

13

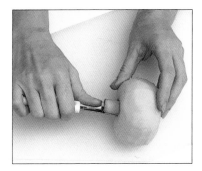

GRATING ZEST FROM CITRUS FRUITS

The outer, coloured zest of citrus fruit, sometimes called the zest, is full of flavor, but the white pith is very bitter. Choose unwaxed fruits and wash and dry the fruit thoroughly before use. Use the fine gauge of a grater and rub the fruit against it to remove the colored zest.

PREPARING SYRUP FOR A SORBET

Water ices and sorbets start with a simple syrup. Heat the sugar and water in a heavy saucepan over medium heat, stirring gently, until all the sugar is dissolved. Bring to a boil, and continue boiling without stirring for 2 minutes or for the time stated.

MAKING AN ICE BOWL

Ice creams and sorbets look spectacular in an ice bowl. Choose two freezerproof bowls, one about 3 inches wider than the other. Pour cold water into the larger bowl to two thirds full, and then center the smaller bowl in the water, weighting it so that it floats level with the big bowl. Keep it in place with masking tape. Add water if necessary, and then freeze, adding flowers or leaves when the water is semi-frozen, if desired. Ease out the small bowl when frozen, release the ice bowl and store in the freezer until needed.

14

TIPS FOR PERFECT ICES

● *The faster you freeze ice cream, the fewer ice crystals will form, so turn the freezer to the coldest setting 1 hour before, or use the fast-freeze facility.*

● *Don't make too much at one time. Not only will this take too long, but it will also result in the formation of larger ice crystals.*

● *Constant churning in an ice-cream maker gives the creamiest results, but whisking by hand when ice crystals start to form, then once or twice more during freezing, is perfectly adequate.*

● *Homemade ice cream freezes hard. Let it soften before serving. This not only makes it easier to scoop but also gives the flavors a chance to develop.*

● *Add chunky flavorings such as chopped preserved ginger, nuts or chocolate chips, when the ice cream is partially frozen, or they will sink.*

● *Use a scoop or baller dipped in lukewarm water for shaping ice cream, or make simple ovals between two teaspoons.*

PREPARING NUTS

To skin whole almonds, blanch them in boiling water for 2 minutes. Drain and cool slightly, then squeeze each to remove the skins. To skin hazelnuts and brazil nuts, toast in a 350°F oven for 10–15 minutes, then rub the nuts in a dish towel to remove the skins.

To oven-toast or broil nuts, spread the nuts evenly on a baking sheet. Toast in a 350°F oven or under the broiler, until golden. Stir occasionally. To fry nuts, put the nuts in a frying pan without fat. Toast over medium heat until golden brown, stirring constantly.

To grind nuts, use a nut mill or coffee grinder and grind a small batch at a time. Don't grind them too much, as they will turn into a paste. You can also grind nuts in a food processor. To prevent turning the nuts into a paste, grind then with some of the sugar or flour used in the recipe.

FLIPPING A CREPE

Crêpes are child's play if you use a good pan, grease it just enough to prevent the batter from sticking, and pour in only enough batter to coat the bottom evenly. As the crêpe sets, shake the pan to keep it from sticking. Check that it is lightly brown underneath, then hold the pan handle firmly, slide the crêpe forward to the opposite rim and flip it over towards you with a neat flick of your wrist. Cook the ciêpe evenly on the second side, before sliding it out onto a plate and serving with your choice of filling.

15

PREPARING A SOUFFLE DISH

To make a cold soufflé that looks as though it has risen above the dish, use a smaller-than-necessary soufflé dish, adding a paper collar to hold the excess mixture in place. Cut a piece of nonstick baking parchment slightly longer than the circumference of the dish and three times its depth. Fold it over lengthwise, wrap it tightly around the outside of the dish and secure it firmly in place with string or freezer tape.

COOK'S TIP

It is not really necessary to make a paper collar for a hot soufflé. Instead, run a clean knife around the edge of the mixture, at a depth of ½-inch, to encourage even rising.

Cold Desserts

Chilled desserts are perfect to make when entertaining, since they can be prepared in advance. Plenty of classic dinner party dishes are included in this selection including Baked Caramel Custard and Minted Raspberry Bavarois, as well as innovative combinations and variations that are sure to impress. Try delicious Poached Pears in Maple-yogurt Sauce and, for the figure-conscious, Grapes in Grape-yogurt Gelatin are a good choice. For everyday family meals try Autumn Pudding, and substitute your choice of seasonal fruits.

Autumn Pudding

INGREDIENTS

10 slices white or whole wheat bread, at least 1 day old
1 Granny Smith apple, peeled, cored and sliced
ripe red plums, halved and pitted
2 cups blackberries
4 tablespoons water
6 tablespoons superfine sugar
yogurt or ricotta cheese, to serve

SERVES 6

1 Slice off the crusts from the bread and use a cookie cutter to cut out a 3-inch round from one slice. Cut all the remaining slices in half.

2 Put the bread circle in the base of a 5-cup heat proof baking dish, then overlap the halves around the sides, saving some for the top.

3 Place the fruit, water and sugar in a pan, heat gently until the sugar dissolves, then simmer for 10 minutes, until soft. Drain, reserving the juice.

4 Spoon the fruit into the dish. Top with the reserved bread and juice.

5 Cover the dish with a saucer and place a weight on top of it. Chill the pudding overnight. Turn out onto a serving plate and serve with yogurt.

Poached Pears in Maple~Yogurt Sauce

INGREDIENTS

6 firm Anjou pears
1 tablespoon lemon juice
1 cup sweet white wine
thinly pared zest of 1 lemon
1 cinnamon stick
2 tablespoons maple syrup
½ teaspoon arrowroot
⅔ cup plain yogurt

SERVES 6

1 Thinly peel the pears, leaving them whole and with the stalks on. Brush with lemon juice, to prevent them from browning. Using a potato peeler or small knife, scoop out the core from the base of each pear and discard it.

2 Place the pears in a wide, heavy saucepan and add the wine, along with enough cold water to almost cover the pears.

3 Add the lemon zest and cinnamon stick, then bring to a boil. Reduce the heat, cover the pan and simmer for about 30–40 minutes, or until all the pears are

tender. Turn them occasionally so that they cook evenly. Lift out the pears carefully, with a large spoon, draining them well.

4 Bring the remaining liquid to a boil. Boil, uncovered, to reduce to about ½ cup. Strain, and add the maple syrup. Blend some of the liquid with the arrowroot. Return to the pan and cook, stirring, until thick and clear. Cool.

5 Slice each pear about three-quarters of the way through, leaving the slices attached at the stem end. Fan out each pear on a serving plate.

6 Stir 2 tablespoons of the cooled syrup into the plain yogurt and spoon it around each pear on the plates. Drizzle with the remaining syrup and serve the pears immediately.

Oranges in Caramel Sauce

3 Using a sharp vegetable knife, slice all the peeled fruit crossways into circles about ½ inch thick. Put the orange slices in a serving bowl and cover them with any leftover juice.

4 Fill a large bowl halfway with cold water and set aside. Place the sugar and 3 tablespoons of water in a small heavy pan without a non-stick coating. Bring it to a boil over high heat, swirling the pan to dissolve all the sugar. Boil, without stirring, until the mixture turns a dark caramel color. Remove the pan from the heat and, standing a safe distance back, dip the base of the pan into the bowl of cold water in order to stop the cooking process.

INGREDIENTS

6 large seedless oranges
½ cup granulated sugar

SERVES 6

1 Using a vegetable peeler, remove wide strips of rind from two of the oranges. Stack two or three strips on top of each other and cut them into very thin julienne strips.

2 Cut a slice from the top and the base of each orange. Cut off the peel in strips from the top to the base, following the contours of the fruit.

5 Add 2 tablespoons water to the caramel, pouring it down the sides of the pan, and swirling it to mix it thoroughly. Add the strips of orange rind and return the pan to the heat. Simmer over medium-low heat for 8–10 minutes until the orange strips are slightly translucent, stirring occasionally.

6 Pour the caramel and rind over the orange slices in the serving bowl, turn gently to mix everything together and chill for at least 1 hour before serving.

Cool Grape Mousse

INGREDIENTS

1½ cups green seedless grapes
2 cups white grape juice
1 packet powdered gelatin
½ cup plain yogurt

SERVES 4

1 Reserve four small sprigs of grapes for decoration and then cut the rest in half.

2 Divide the grapes between four stemmed glasses and tilt the glasses to one side, propping them firmly in a bowl of ice.

3 Place the grape juice in a saucepan and heat it until almost boiling. Remove the pan from the heat and add the gelatin, stirring until it dissolves.

4 Pour half the grape juice over the grapes in the tilted glasses and allow to set.

5 Cool the remaining grape juice slightly, then stir it into the yogurt.

6 Stand the four set glasses upright and divide the yogurt mixture among them. Chill until set, about two hours, then top each one with a sprig of grapes before serving.

Apples & Raspberries in Rose Tea Syrup

INGREDIENTS

1 teaspoon rose tea
1 teaspoon rose water (optional)
¼ cup granulated sugar
1 teaspoon lemon juice
5 apples
1 cup fresh raspberries

SERVES 4

1 Make the tea using 3¾ cups of boiling water together with the rose water, if using. Let steep for 4 minutes.

2 Place the sugar and lemon juice in a large stainless steel saucepan. Carefully strain in all the infused rose tea and stir well until the sugar dissolves.

3 Peel, core and quarter the apples. Poach them in the syrup for about 5 minutes, then transfer the apples and syrup to a large baking sheet and let cool.

4 Pour the cooled apples and rose syrup into a mixing bowl and add the fresh raspberries. Mix well to combine all the ingredients, then spoon the fruit mixture into individual serving dishes or bowls and serve at room temperature.

COOK'S TIP

If fresh raspberries are out of season, use the same weight of frozen fruit or one 14-ounce can fruit, drained well.

22

Fresh Fruit with Mango Sauce

INGREDIENTS

1 large ripe mango, peeled, pitted and cubed
rind of 1 orange
juice of 3 oranges
superfine sugar, to taste
2 peaches
2 nectarines
1 small mango, peeled
2 plums
1 pear or ½ small melon
juice of 1 lemon
¼ cup wild strawberries
¼ cup raspberries
¼ cup blueberries
small mint sprigs, to decorate

SERVES 6

1 In a food processor fitted with a metal blade, process the large mango until smooth. Add the orange rind, juice and sugar to taste and process again until very smooth. Press through a strainer into a bowl. Chill the sauce until needed.

2 Peel the peaches, then pit and slice the peaches, nectarines, small mango and plums. Peel and quarter the pear, if using, and remove the core. Alternately, seed and slice the half melon thinly and remove all the peel.

3 Place all the sliced fruits on a large plate and sprinkle with the lemon juice to prevent them from discoloring. Chill the plate of fruit, covered with clear plastic wrap, for up to 3 hours before serving.

4 To serve the fruit, arrange the slices on individual serving plates and spoon the strawberries, raspberries and blueberries over the top. Drizzle with a little of the fresh mango sauce and decorate the plates with mint sprigs. Serve the remaining mango sauce separately.

24

Cowslip Syllabub

INGREDIENTS

7 fluid ounces white wine
¼ cup superfine sugar
finely grated zest of 1 orange
juice of 1 orange
½ pint heavy cream
32 cowslip flowers, fresh or crystallized
8 viola flowers, fresh or crystallized
fresh mint sprigs, to decorate
langue de chat cookies, to serve

SERVES 6

1 To make the syllabub, place the wine, sugar, orange zest and orange juice in a bowl. Let the mixture stand for at least 2 hours.

2 Add the mixture to the cream a little at a time, whisking constantly, until it stands in soft peaks. Spoon a little of the syllabub into the base of six serving glasses, and sprinkle a few of the cowslips and violas around the edges.

3 Continue to spoon the syllabub into the glasses to form a peak in the center. Sprinkle on more flowers and chill in the refrigerator. Attach any remaining flowers to the langue de chat cookies with a dab of icing, and serve the syllabub with the decorated cookies.

4 For the crystallized flowers, coat the petals with a thin, even layer of lightly beaten egg whites. Use tweezers to dip the flowers into the egg whites. The process must be done quickly before the egg white dries.

5 Sprinkle sifted confectioners' sugar over the flowers, shaking off any excess. Uneven patches create an attractive light and dark shade contrast, but the flowers will not be preserved as efficiently.

6 Let the coated flowers dry. Store carefully between layers of tissue paper in a cool, dry place, for up to a week. Do not refrigerate the petals.

Baked Caramel Custard

INGREDIENTS

1 ¼ cups sugar
4 tablespoons water
1 vanilla pod
1 ⅔ cups milk
1 cup heavy or whipping cream
5 large eggs
2 egg yolks

SERVES 6–8

1 Put ¾ cup of the sugar in a small heavy saucepan with the water to moisten. Bring to a boil over high heat, swirling the pan until the sugar dissolves. Boil rapidly, without stirring, until the syrup turns a dark caramel color (this will take about 4–5 minutes).

2 Immediately pour the caramel into a 4-cup soufflé dish. Holding the dish with oven mitts, quickly swirl it to coat the base and sides with the caramel and set aside. (The caramel will harden quickly as it cools.) Place the dish in a small roasting pan. Preheat the oven to 325°F.

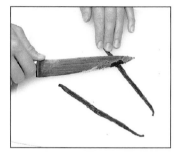

3 Split the vanilla pod lengthwise and scrape the black seeds into a saucepan. Add the milk and cream. Bring to a boil over medium-high heat, stirring frequently. Remove the pan from the heat, cover and set aside for 15–20 minutes.

4 In a bowl, whisk the eggs and egg yolks with the remaining sugar for 2–3 minutes until smooth and creamy. Whisk in the hot milk. Strain the mixture into the caramel-lined dish. Cover with foil.

5 Pour enough boiling water into the roasting pan to come halfway up the sides of the dish. Bake the custard for 40–45 minutes until a knife inserted about 2 inches from the edge comes out clean (the custard should be just set). Remove from the roasting pan and cool for at least 30 minutes, then chill overnight.

6 To serve, carefully run a sharp knife around the edge of the dish to loosen the custard. Cover the dish with a plate. Holding them both tightly, invert the dish and plate together. Gently lift one edge of the dish, allowing the caramel to run over the sides, then slowly lift off the dish.

Minted Raspberry Bavarois

Ingredients

*3 cups fresh or frozen and
thawed raspberries
2 tablespoons confectioners' sugar
2 tablespoons lemon juice
1 tablespoon finely chopped fresh mint
2 tablespoons powdered gelatin
5 tablespoons boiling water
1¼ cups custard
1¼ cups plain yogurt
fresh mint sprigs, to garnish*

Serves 6

3 Sprinkle I teaspoon of the gelatin over 2 tablespoons of boiling water and stir until it has dissolved. Add it to ⅔ cup of the raspberry purée.

4 Pour this jelly into a 4-cup mold, and leave the mold to chill in the fridge until the jelly is just on the point of setting. Tip the mold to swirl the jelly around the sides, then leave to chill until the jelly has set completely.

1 Reserve some raspberries for decoration. Place the rest with the confectioners' sugar and lemon juice in a food processor or blender. Process until smooth.

5 Stir the rest of the fruit purée into the custard with the yogurt. Dissolve the rest of the gelatin in the rest of the water and stir it into the fruit mixture.

2 Pass the purée through a strainer to remove the raspberry seeds. Add the chopped fresh mint. You should have about 2½ cups of purée.

6 Pour the custard into the mold and let chill until it has set. To serve, dip the mold quickly into hot water, then turn it out and decorate it with the reserved raspberries and the mint sprigs.

30

Baked Custard with Burnt Sugar

INGREDIENTS

1 vanilla pod
4 cups heavy or whipping cream
6 egg yolks
½ cup superfine sugar
2 tablespoons almond or orange liqueur
6 tablespoons light brown sugar

SERVES 6

1 Preheat the oven to 300°F. Place six ½-cup ramekins in a large roasting pan or heat proof dish and set aside.

2 Using a small sharp knife, split the vanilla pod lengthwise and scrape the black seeds into a pan. Add the pod, then add the cream and bring just to a boil over medium-high heat, stirring frequently. Remove from the heat and cover. Set aside for about 15–20 minutes. Remove the vanilla pod.

3 In a bowl, whisk the egg yolks with the superfine sugar and liqueur until well blended. Whisk in the hot cream and strain into a large bowl. Divide among the ramekins.

4 Pour enough boiling water into the roasting pan to come halfway up the sides of the ramekin dishes. Cover the pan with foil and bake for about 30 minutes in the preheated oven until the custards are just set. Remove from the pan and leave to cool. Empty the water from the roasting pan, replace the ramekins and set aside to chill.

5 Preheat the broiler. Sprinkle the light brown sugar evenly over the surface of each custard and broil for 30–60 seconds until the sugar melts and caramelizes. (Do not let the sugar burn or the custard curdle.) Serve immediately.

Cherry Pudding

INGREDIENTS

1 pound ripe cherries
2 tablespoons kirsch or fruit brandy or
1 tablespoon lemon juice
1 tablespoon confectioners' sugar
3 tablespoons unbleached all-purpose flour
3 tablespoons granulated sugar
¾ cup milk or cream
2 eggs
grated zest of ½ lemon
pinch of freshly grated nutmeg
¼ teaspoon vanilla extract

SERVES 4

1 Pit the ripe cherries. Combine them in a mixing bowl with the kirsch, fruit brandy or lemon juice and confectioners' sugar. Set aside for about 1–2 hours.

2 Preheat the oven to 375°F. Generously butter an 10-inch oval gratin dish or other shallow heat proof dish.

3 Sift the flour into a bowl. Add the sugar. Slowly whisk in the milk until smoothly blended. Add the eggs, lemon zest, nutmeg and vanilla extract and whisk until well combined and smooth.

4 Scatter the cherries evenly in the baking dish. Pour on the batter and bake in the preheated oven for 45 minutes, or until the pudding is set and puffed

around the edges; it is ready when a knife inserted in the center comes out clean. Serve either warm or at room temperature.

Chocolate, Date & Walnut Pudding

INGREDIENTS

2 tablespoons chopped walnuts
2 tablespoons chopped dates
2 eggs
1 teaspoon vanilla extract
2 tablespoons superfine sugar
3 tablespoons whole wheat flour
1 tablespoon unsweetened cocoa powder
2 tablespoons milk

SERVES 4

1 First, grease a 5-cup heat proof baking dish or mixing bowl and place a small circle of baking parchment paper or wax paper in the bottom. Spoon in all the chopped walnuts and dates. Preheat the oven to 350°F.

2 Separate the eggs and place the yolks in a mixing bowl with the vanilla extract and sugar. Place the bowl over a pan of hot water and whisk until the mixture is thick and pale.

3 Sift the flour and cocoa into the mixture and fold them in lightly. Stir in the milk, to moisten the mixture slightly. Whisk the egg whites until they hold soft peaks and fold them in.

4 Spoon the mixture into the basin and bake for 40–45 minutes, or until risen and firm to the touch. Serve immediately.

37

Creole Bread & Butter Pudding

INGREDIENTS

4 dried apricots, chopped
1 tablespoon raisins
2 tablespoons golden raisins
1 tablespoon chopped candied citrus peel
1 loaf French bread, thinly sliced
4 tablespoons butter, melted
½ cup superfine sugar
3 eggs
½ teaspoon vanilla extract
2 cups milk
⅔ cup heavy or whipping cream
2 tablespoons rum
SAUCE
⅔ cup heavy or whipping cream
2 tablespoons plain yogurt
1-2 tablespoons rum
1 tablespoon superfine sugar

SERVES 4–6

38

2 Whisk together the sugar, eggs and vanilla extract. Heat the milk and cream until just boiling and whisk into the eggs. Strain over the bread and fruit.  Sprinkle the rum on top. Press the bread down, cover with foil and leave for 20 minutes.

1 Preheat the oven to 350°F. Lightly butter a deep 6-cup heat proof baking dish. Mix the dried fruits with the mixed peel and sprinkle a little in the dish. Brush both sides of the bread slices with melted butter. Fill the dish with alternate layers of bread and dried fruit, finishing with a layer of bread.

3 Bake in a roasting pan half filled with boiling water for 1 hour or until the custard is set. Remove the foil and cook for 10 minutes more, until golden.

4 Warm all the sauce ingredients together in a small pan, stirring gently. Serve alongside the hot pudding.

Plum Pie

INGREDIENTS

2½ cups flour
1 teaspoon salt
⅓ cup refrigerated sweet butter
½ cup refrigerated shortening
4-8 tablespoons iced water
milk, for glazing
FILLING
2 pounds red or purple plums, halved and pitted
grated rind of 1 lemon
1 tablespoon lemon juice
½-¾ cup sugar
3 tablespoons quick-cooking tapioca
pinch of salt
½ teaspoon ground cinnamon
¼ teaspoon grated nutmeg

SERVES 8

39

1 Sift the flour and salt into a bowl. Rub in the butter and shortening until the mixture resembles breadcrumbs. Stir in just enough iced water to bind the pastry. Gather into two balls, one slightly larger than the other. Wrap, and refrigerate for 20 minutes.

2 Preheat the oven to 425°F. Line a cookie sheet with wax paper. Set it aside. Roll out the larger piece of pastry to a thickness of about ⅛ inch, and line a 9-inch pie pan.

3 Roll out the smaller piece of pastry to a round slightly larger than the top of the pie. Support it on the prepared cookie sheet, then stamp out four hearts from the center of the pastry, using a cutter. Reserve the pastry hearts.

4 Make the filling by mixing all the ingredients in a bowl. Use the larger quantity of sugar if the plums are very tart. Spoon the filling into the pastry shell, then lift the pastry on the wax paper, and slide it into position over the filling. Trim, and pinch to seal. Arrange the cut-out pastry hearts on top. Glaze the top of the pie with milk, and bake for 15 minutes. Lower the oven temperature to 350°F, and bake for 30–35 minutes more, protecting the top with foil if needed.

Blackberry Cobbler

INGREDIENTS

6 cups blackberries
1 cup superfine sugar
3 tablespoons unbleached all-purpose flour
grated zest of 1 lemon
2 tablespoons sugar mixed with
¼ teaspoon grated nutmeg
TOPPING
2 cups unbleached all-purpose flour
1 cup superfine sugar
1 tablespoon baking powder
¼ teaspoon salt
1 cup milk
½ cup butter, melted

SERVES 8

1 First preheat the oven to 350°F. In a mixing bowl, combine all the blackberries with the superfine sugar, flour and lemon zest. Stir gently to blend together before transferring to a 10-cup heat proof baking dish.

2 To make the topping, sift the flour, sugar, baking powder, and salt into a large bowl. Set aside. Combine the milk and butter in a large measuring cup.

3 Gradually stir the butter and milk mixture into the dry ingredients in the bowl and stir with a wooden spoon until the batter becomes smooth.

4 Spoon the batter over the fruit mixture, spreading it right to the edges. Sprinkle with the sugar and nutmeg mixture, then bake in the preheated oven for about 50 minutes, until the topping is set and lightly browned. Serve hot.

Apple Soufflé Omelette

42

INGREDIENTS

4 eggs, separated
2 tablespoons cream
1 tablespoon superfine sugar
1 tablespoon butter
confectioners' sugar, to decorate
FILLING
1 Granny Smith apple, peeled, cored and sliced
2 tablespoons butter
2 tablespoons light brown sugar
3 tablespoons cream

SERVES 2

1 For the filling, gently sauté the apple slices in the butter and sugar until just tender. Stir in the cream and keep warm while you make the omelette.

2 Place the egg yolks in a bowl with the cream and sugar and beat well. Whisk the egg whites until stiff, then fold into the yolk mixture.

3 Melt the butter in a large heavy frying pan and pour in the soufflé mixture, spreading it evenly. Cook for 1 minute until golden underneath, then place under a hot broiler and brown the top.

4 Slide the omelette onto a plate, top with the apple filling, then fold the omelette in half. Sift confectioners' sugar liberally over the omelette, and serve immediately.

COOK'S TIP

For a summer variation, use fresh raspberries or strawberries instead of apples.

Plum Filo Pockets

INGREDIENTS

½ cup ricotta cheese
1 tablespoon raw sugar
½ teaspoon ground cloves
8 large firm plums, halved and pitted
8 sheets filo pastry
sunflower oil, for brushing
confectioners' sugar, to decorate

SERVES 4

1 First, preheat the oven to 425°F and then combine the ricotta cheese, raw sugar and ground cloves in a small bowl. Stir well until combined.

2 Sandwich the plum halves back together with a spoonful of the cheese mixture. Cut the filo sheets into 16 pieces, about 9 inches square. Brush one lightly with oil and place a second on top diagonally. Repeat with the other squares.

3 Put a plum on each square and wrap the pastry around it, pinching the corners together. Bake for 15–18 minutes until golden. Dust with confectioners' sugar.

43

Fruity Bread Pudding

44

INGREDIENTS

½ cup mixed dried fruit
⅔ cup apple juice
4 ounces stale whole wheat or white bread, diced
1 teaspoon pumpkin pie spice
1 large banana, sliced
⅔ cup milk
1 tablespoon raw sugar
plain yogurt, to serve

SERVES 4

1 Preheat the oven to 400°F. Place the dried fruit in a saucepan with the apple juice and bring to a boil.

2 Quickly remove the pan from the heat and carefully stir in the bread, spices and sliced banana. Mix well. Spoon this mixture into a shallow 5-cup heat proof baking dish. Then pour the milk evenly over the top of the mixture.

3 Sprinkle the top with the raw sugar and bake 25–30 minutes, until it is set and golden brown. Serve hot or cold, with yogurt.

COOK'S TIP

Different types of bread and their degree of staleness will cause variation in the amount of liquid absorbed, so you may need to adjust the amount of milk to allow for this.

Gingerbread Upside-Down Pudding

INGREDIENTS

1 tablespoon light brown sugar
4 peaches, halved and pitted, or 8 canned
peach halves
8 walnut halves
yogurt or whipped cream, to serve
BASE
1 cup whole wheat flour
1 1/2 teaspoons ground ginger
1/2 teaspoon baking soda
1 teaspoon ground cinnamon
1/2 cup dark brown sugar
1 egg
1/2 cup milk
1/4 cup sunflower oil

SERVES 4–6

2 Arrange the peach halves, cut-side down, in the pan with a walnut half in each.

3 Make the base. Sift together the flour, ginger, baking soda, and cinnamon, then stir in the sugar. Beat together the egg, milk and oil, then mix into the dry ingredients until smooth.

4 Pour the mixture evenly over the peaches and bake for 35–40 minutes, until firm to the touch. Release onto a serving plate. Serve hot with yogurt or whipped cream.

45

1 First, preheat the oven to 350°F and brush the bottom and sides of a 9-inch round springform pan with oil. Sprinkle the sugar over the bottom.

Cherry Lattice Pie

INGREDIENTS

2 cups all-purpose flour
1 teaspoon salt
¾ cup butter or margarine, diced
4-5 tablespoons ice water
FILLING
1-pound can cherries, drained, or
4 cups pitted fresh cherries
6 tablespoons sugar
¼ cup flour
1½ tablespoons fresh lemon juice
¼ teaspoon almond extract
2 tablespoons butter or margarine

SERVES 8

1 Make the pastry. Sift the flour and salt into a mixing bowl. Rub in the butter or margarine until the mixture resembles coarse bread crumbs. Sprinkle in the ice water, 1 tablespoon at a time, tossing with your fingertips until the dough forms a ball.

2 Divide the dough in half and shape each half into a ball. On a lightly floured surface, roll out one of the balls to a circle about 12 inches in diameter.

3 Use the dough circle to line a 9-inch pie pan, easing the dough in and being careful not to stretch it. Trim all the excess dough, leaving a ½-inch overhang around the rim. Roll out the remaining dough to ⅛-inch thickness. With a sharp knife, cut out 11 strips, ½ inch wide.

4 In a mixing bowl, combine the cherries, sugar, flour, lemon juice and almond extract. Spoon the mixture into the pastry shell and dot the butter or margarine over the surface.

5 For the lattice, space five of the pastry strips over the cherry filling and fold every other strip back. Lay a strip across, perpendicular to the others. Fold  the strips back over the filling. Continue in this way, folding back every other strip each time you add a cross strip. Trim the ends of the lattice strips to make them even with the pastry overhang Press together so that the edge rests on the rim of the pan. Flute the edge. Chill for 15 minutes. Preheat the oven to 425°F.

6 Bake the pie for 30 minutes, covering the edge with foil, if necessary, to prevent burning.

Cherry Crêpes

Ingredients

CRÊPES
1/2 cup unbleached all-purpose flour
1/2 cup whole wheat flour
pinch of salt
1 egg white
2/3 cup milk
2/3 cup water
a little oil, for frying
ricotta cheese, to serve
FILLING
15-ounce can black cherries in juice
1 1/2 teaspoons arrowroot

SERVES 4

1 Sift the flours and salt into a bowl.

2 Make a well in the center of the flour and add the egg white. Gradually beat in the milk and water, whisking hard until all the flour and liquid is incorporated and the batter is smooth and bubbly.

3 Heat a non-stick pan with a small amount of oil until it is very hot. Pour in just enough batter to cover the base of the pan and swirl to cover it evenly.

4 Cook until the crêpe is set and golden, and then turn to cook the other side. Remove to a paper towel and repeat with the remaining batter, to make about eight crêpes in all.

5 Drain the cherries, reserving the juice. Blend about 2 tablespoons of the juice from the can of cherries with the arrowroot in a saucepan. Stir in the rest of the juice. Heat gently, stirring, until boiling. Stir the mixture over medium heat for about 2 minutes, until thickened and clear.

6 Add the cherries to the pan and stir until heated through. Spoon the cherry mixture into the crêpes, fold them in quarters and serve with ricotta cheese.

48

Amaretto Soufflé

INGREDIENTS

butter, for greasing
½ cup superfine sugar, plus extra
6 amaretti cookies, coarsely crushed
6 tablespoons Amaretto
4 eggs, separated, plus 1 egg white
for sprinkling
tablespoons unbleached all-purpose flour
1 cup milk
pinch of cream of tartar (optional)
confectioners' sugar, for decorating

SERVES 6

1 Preheat the oven to 400°F. Butter a 6-cup soufflé dish and sprinkle with superfine sugar. Sprinkle the cookies with 2 tablespoons of the Amaretto and set aside.

2 Mix the 4 egg yolks with 2 tablespoons of the superfine sugar and the flour. Stir until smooth. Put the milk in a heavy saucepan and bring it just to a boil. Remove from the heat and gradually add the hot milk to the beaten egg mixture, stirring.

3 Pour the milk and egg mixture back into the pan. Set it over medium-low heat and simmer gently for 4 minutes or until thickened, stirring constantly. Add the remaining Amaretto and remove the pan from the heat.

4 In a scrupulously clean, grease-free bowl, whisk the 5 egg whites until they form soft peaks. (If not using a copper bowl, add the cream of tartar as soon as the whites are frothy.) Add the remaining sugar and continue whisking until stiff.

5 Add about one-quarter of the whites to the Amaretto mixture and stir in with a rubber spatula. Add the remaining whites and fold in gently.

6 Spoon half the mixture into the prepared dish. Cover with a layer of the moistened amaretti cookies, then spoon the remaining soufflé mixture evenly on the top.

7 Bake the dish for 20 minutes in the preheated oven, or until the soufflé is risen and lightly browned on top. Sprinkle with sifted confectioners' sugar and serve immediately.

Pear & Blueberry Pie

INGREDIENTS

2 cups all-purpose flour
pinch of salt
4 tablespoons Crisco, cubed
4 tablespoons butter, cubed
FILLING
6 cups blueberries
2 tablespoons sugar
1 tablespoon arrowroot
2 ripe but firm pears, peeled, cored and sliced
½ teaspoon ground cinnamon
grated rind of ½ lemon
beaten egg, to glaze
sugar, for sprinkling
sour cream, to serve

SERVES 4

1 Sift the flour and salt into a bowl and rub in the shortening. Stir in 3 tablespoons cold water and mix to a dough. Chill for 30 minutes.

2 Place 2 cups of the blueberries in a pan with the sugar. Cover and cook gently until the blueberries have softened. Press through a sieve.

3 Blend the arrowroot with 2 tablespoons cold water and add to the blueberry purée. Place in a small saucepan and bring to a boil, stirring until thickened. Cool the mixture slightly.

4 Place a baking sheet in the oven and preheat to 375°F. Roll out just over half the pastry on a lightly floured surface and use to line an 8-inch shallow pie pan or a heat proof plate; do this by flopping the pastry over the rolling pin and lifting it into position. Let the edges overhang.

5 Combine the remaining blueberries, the pears, cinnamon and lemon rind and spoon into the tin. Pour the blueberry purée over the top.

6 Roll out the remaining pastry to just larger than the pie tin and lay it over the filling. Press the edges together to seal, then trim off any excess pastry and crimp the edge. Make a small slit in the center to allow steam to escape. Brush with egg and sprinkle with sugar. Bake the pie on the hot baking sheet for 40–45 minutes, or until golden. Serve warm with sour cream.

Baked Blackberry Cheesecake

INGREDIENTS

¾ cup cottage cheese
⅔ cup low-fat plain yogurt
1 tablespoon whole-wheat flour
2 tablespoons sugar
1 egg
1 egg white
finely grated zest and juice of ½ lemon
2 cups fresh or frozen and thawed blackberries

SERVES 5

54

4 Transfer the mixture to the prepared pan and bake it for 30–35 minutes or until just set. Turn off the oven and let sit for another 30 minutes.

1 First, preheat the oven to 350°F. Then lightly grease and line the bottom of a fluted 7-inch tart pan.

2 Place the cottage cheese in a food processor and process until smooth. Alternatively, rub it through a sieve to obtain a smooth mixture.

3 Add the yogurt, flour, sugar, egg and egg white and mix. Add the lemon zest, juice and blackberries, reserving a few for decoration.

5 Run a knife around the edge of the cheesecake and then turn it out. Remove the lining paper and place the cheesecake on a warm serving plate.

6 Decorate the cheesecake with the reserved blackberries and serve it warm.

Chocolate & Coffee Desserts

Rich, creamy, chocolate desserts are sure winners whatever the occasion. This indulgent ingredient is guaranteed to turn any dish into a wicked temptation. Try Chocolate Cheesecake Pie decorated with swirls of whipped cream and curls of solid semi-sweet or milk chocolate, or team this heavenly ingredient with the unmistakable flavor of coffee. Chocolate Cake with Coffee Sauce successfully combines the two flavors and makes a feast for a special occasion. For a rich and smooth dessert, try Luxury Mocha Mousse served with chocolate coffee beans.

French Chocolate Cake

INGREDIENTS

1 cup unsalted butter, cut into pieces
9 ounces good-quality semisweet chocolate, chopped
½ cup granulated sugar
2 tablespoons brandy or orange-flavor liqueur
5 eggs
1 tablespoon unbleached all-purpose flour
confectioners' sugar, to decorate
sour cream and fresh cherries, to serve

SERVES 10

58

1 Preheat the oven to 350°F. Line the bottom of a 9-inch springform pan with a circle of baking parchment. Wrap foil around the pan so it is water-tight.

2 Stir the butter, chocolate and granulated sugar over low heat until smooth. Cool slightly. Stir in the liqueur. In a bowl, beat the eggs lightly, then beat in the flour. Slowly beat in the chocolate mixture to blend. Pour into the pan. Smooth the surface.

3 Place the springform pan in a roasting pan. Fill the roasting pan with enough boiling water to come ¾ inch up the side of the springform pan. Bake for 25–30 minutes, until the edge of the cake is set, but the center is still soft. Remove the foil. Cool in the pan on a wire rack (the cake will sink and may crack).

4 Turn the cake upside-down onto a wire rack. Release the springform pan and remove the paper. The bottom of the cake is now the top.

5 Cut 6–8 strips of baking parchment 1 inch wide and place them randomly over the cake, or make a lattice-style pattern if you wish. Dust the cake with confectioners' sugar, then carefully remove the paper. Slide the cake onto a serving plate and serve with sour cream and fresh cherries.

Coffee Jellies with Amaretti Cream

INGREDIENTS

6 tablespoons superfine sugar
2 cups strong hot coffee
2-3 tablespoons dark rum or Kahlua
4 teaspoons powdered gelatin
COFFEE AMARETTI CREAM
⅔ cup heavy or whipping cream
1 tablespoon confectioners' sugar, sifted
2-3 teaspoons instant coffee powder
dissolved in 1 tablespoon hot water
6 large amaretti cookies, crushed

SERVES 4

1 Put the sugar in a saucepan with 5 tablespoons of water and stir over gentle heat until dissolved. Increase the heat; allow the syrup to boil steadily, without stirring, for 3–4 minutes.

2 Stir all the hot coffee and rum or Kahlua into the hot syrup. Sprinkle the powdered gelatin over the top and stir until it dissolves completely.

3 Pour the coffee mixture into four parfait glasses and allow them to cool thoroughly, before placing them in the fridge. Leave the glasses in the fridge for several hours until they are completely set.

4 To make the amaretti cream, lightly whip the cream with the confectioners' sugar until it holds stiff peaks. Stir in the instant coffee, then 2 tablespoons of the crushed amaretti cookies.

5 Remove the jellies from the refrigerator. Spoon a little of the coffee amaretti cream on top of the parfaits. Top with the reserved amaretti cookie crumbs and serve the dessert immediately.

59

White Chocolate Cheesecake

INGREDIENTS

5 ounces (about 16-18) graham crackers
½ cup blanched hazelnuts, toasted
4 tablespoons unsalted butter, melted
½ teaspoon ground cinnamon
FILLING
12 ounces good quality white chocolate, chopped
½ cup heavy or whipping cream
3 packages (8 ounces each) cream cheese, softened
¼ cup granulated sugar
4 eggs
1 tablespoon vanilla extract
TOPPING
2 cups sour cream
¼ cup granulated sugar
1 tablespoon hazelnut-flavor liqueur or 1 teaspoon vanilla extract
white chocolate curls, to decorate
unsweetened cocoa powder, for dusting (optional)

SERVES 16–20

1 Preheat the oven to 350°F and grease a 9-inch springform pan. Process the graham crackers and hazelnuts to fine crumbs, then mix with the butter and cinnamon. Press the mixture onto the bottom and sides of the pan and bake for 5–7 minutes, or until just set.

2 Lower the oven to 300°F. Make the filling. Melt the chocolate and cream over low heat until smooth, stirring frequently. Cool.

3 Beat the cream cheese and sugar until smooth; beat in the eggs, one at a time, the white chocolate mixture and the vanilla. Pour into the baked crust and bake for 45–55 minutes, or until the edge of the filling is firm but the center is still slightly soft. Transfer to a wire rack, still in the pan, and increase the oven temperature to 400°F.

4 Make the topping. Whisk the sour cream with the sugar and vanilla and pour it over the cheesecake, spreading it evenly. Return the cheesecake to the oven for 5–7 minutes. Turn off the oven, but do not open the door for 1 hour.

5 Transfer the cheesecake to a wire rack to cool in the pan. Remove the pan, then chill the cheesecake, loosely covered, overnight.

6 Place the cheesecake on a serving plate. Decorate the top with chocolate curls and dust lightly with cocoa, if desired.

Chocolate Pavlova with Chocolate Curls

INGREDIENTS

2½ cups confectioners' sugar
1 tablespoon unsweetened cocoa powder
1 teaspoon cornstarch
5 egg whites, at room temperature
pinch of salt
1 teaspoon cider vinegar or lemon juice
CHOCOLATE CREAM
6 ounces good quality semisweet chocolate, chopped
½ cup milk
2 tablespoons butter, cut into pieces
2 tablespoons brandy
2 cups heavy or whipping cream
TOPPING
4 cups mixed berries or diced mango, papaya, lychees and pineapple
chocolate curls
confectioners' sugar

SERVES 8–10

1 Preheat the oven to 325°F. Place a sheet of baking parchment onto a baking sheet and mark an 8-inch circle on it. Sift 3 tablespoons of the confectioners' sugar with the cocoa and cornstarch and set aside. Using an electric mixer, beat the egg whites until frothy. Add the salt and beat until the whites form stiff peaks.

2 Sprinkle the remaining confectioners' sugar into the egg whites, a little at a time, making sure each addition is blended in before beating in the next. Fold in the cornstarch mixture, then quickly fold in the vinegar or lemon juice.

3 Now spoon the mixture onto the paper circle, with the sides higher than the center. Bake for 1 hour, until set, then turn off the oven but leave the meringue  inside for 1 hour longer. Remove from the oven, peel off the paper and let cool.

4 Make the chocolate cream. Melt the chocolate in the milk over low heat, stirring until smooth. Remove from the heat and whisk in the butter and brandy. Cool for 1 hour.

5 Transfer the meringue to a serving plate. When the chocolate mixture has cooled, but is not too firm, beat the cream until soft peaks form. Stir half the cream into the chocolate mixture to lighten it, then fold in the remaining cream. Spoon it into the center of the meringue. Arrange fruit and chocolate curls in the center of the meringue, on top of the cream. Dust with confectioners' sugar and serve.

Chocolate Cream Puffs

INGREDIENTS

1 cup water
½ teaspoon salt
1 tablespoon granulated sugar
½ cup unsalted butter, cut into pieces
¼ cups unbleached all-purpose flour, sifted
2 tablespoons unsweetened cocoa powder, sifted
4-5 eggs
1 recipe Chocolate Cream (page 62),
for filling
GLAZE
1¼ cups heavy or whipping cream
4 tablespoons unsalted butter, cut into pieces
1 tablespoon corn syrup
8 ounces good quality bittersweet chocolate,
chopped
1 teaspoon vanilla extract

MAKES 12

1 Preheat the oven to 425°F. Grease a baking sheet. Bring the water, salt, sugar and butter to a boil. Remove from the heat; add the flour and cocoa. Stir vigorously until the mixture pulls away from the sides of the pan. Heat for 1 minute, beating constantly. Remove from the heat.

2 Beat in four of the eggs, one at a time. The mixture should be thick, smooth and shiny and fall from a spoon. If it is too dry, beat the fifth egg separate-

ly, then add it to the mixture gradually. Spoon the batter into an icing bag with a star tip and pipe 12 puffs on the baking sheet.

3 Bake the puffs for 35–40 minutes until puffed and golden. Slice off the top third of each puff and return both tops and bottoms, cut side up, to the baking sheet. Return them to the oven for a few more minutes. Cool on a wire rack.

4 Spoon the chocolate cream into a piping bag fitted with a plain tip. Fill the bottom of each puff, then cover with a top.

5 Make the glaze. Melt the cream, butter, syrup, chocolate and vanilla until smooth, stirring often. Remove from the heat and let cool for about 20–30 minutes, until slightly thickened. Pour a little glaze over each of the cream puffs, or dip the top of each puff into the glaze, and let set. To serve, arrange the puffs on a serving plate in a single layer or pile them up on top of each other.

Chocolate Loaf with Coffee Sauce

INGREDIENTS

*6 ounces good quality semisweet chocolate,
chopped
4 tablespoons butter, softened
4 large eggs, separated
2 tablespoons rum or brandy (optional)
pinch of cream of tartar
chocolate curls and chocolate-covered
coffee beans, to decorate*
COFFEE SAUCE
*2½ cups milk
9 egg yolks
¼ cup superfine sugar
1 teaspoon vanilla extract
1 tablespoon instant coffee powder, dissolved
in 2 tablespoons hot water*

SERVES 6–8

1 Line a 5-cup loaf pan with plastic wrap. Place the semisweet chocolate in a bowl placed over hot water and leave for 3–5 minutes, then stir.

2 Remove the bowl from the pan and quickly beat in the butter, egg yolks, one at a time, and rum or brandy, if using.

3 In a clean grease-free bowl, using an electric mixer, beat the egg whites slowly until frothy. Add the cream of tartar, increase the speed and continue beating until they form stiff peaks. Stir one-third of the egg whites into the chocolate mixture, then fold in the remaining whites. Pour into the lined loaf pan and smooth the top. Cover and freeze for 2–3 hours, until set.

4 Make the coffee sauce. Bring the milk to a simmer over medium heat. Whisk together the egg yolks and the superfine sugar for 2–3 minutes until thick and creamy, then whisk in the hot milk and return the mixture to the saucepan. With a wooden spoon, stir over low heat until the sauce begins to thicken and coat the back of the spoon. Strain the custard into a chilled bowl, stir in the vanilla extract and coffee and set aside to cool, stirring occasionally. Chill.

5 To serve, uncover the loaf pan and dip the bottom into hot water for 10 seconds. Invert the chocolate loaf onto a board and peel off the plastic wrap. Cut the loaf into slices and serve topped with the coffee sauce. Decorate with the chocolate curls and chocolate-covered coffee beans.

66

Hazelnut Meringue Torte with Pears

INGREDIENTS

¾ cup granulated sugar
1 vanilla pod, split
2 cups water
4 ripe pears, peeled, halved and cored
6 egg whites
2½ cups confectioners' sugar
1¼ cups ground hazelnuts
1 teaspoon vanilla extract
2 ounces good quality semisweet chocolate, melted
chocolate caraque, to decorate
CHOCOLATE CREAM
2 cups whipping cream
10 ounces good-quality semisweet chocolate, melted
4 tablespoons hazelnut-flavor liqueur

SERVES 8–10

1 In a pan large enough to hold the pears in a single layer, combine the sugar, vanilla pod and water. Bring to a boil, stirring until the sugar dissolves. Reduce the heat and add the pears. Cover and simmer for 12–15 minutes until tender. Remove from heat and let cool. Preheat the oven to 350°F.

2 Draw a 9-inch circle on two sheets of baking parchment and place on two baking sheets.

3 Whisk the egg whites until soft peaks form, then gradually add the confectioners' sugar, whisking until stiff and glossy. Gently fold in the nuts and vanilla and spoon the meringue onto the marked circles. Bake for 1 hour. Turn off the heat and cool in the oven.

4 Slice the pear halves lengthwise. Then, make the chocolate cream. Beat the cream into soft peaks, then fold in the melted chocolate and liqueur. Put a third of the chocolate cream into an icing bag fitted with a star tip. Spread one meringue layer with half the remaining chocolate cream and top with half the pears. Pipe rosettes around the edge.

5 Top with the second meringue and the remaining chocolate cream and pear slices. Pipe rosettes around the edge. Drizzle the melted chocolate over the pears and decorate with the chocolate shavings. Chill for 1 hour before serving.

Iced Praline Torte

INGREDIENTS

1 cup blanched almonds
½ cup water
1½ cups sugar
⅔ cup raisins
6 tablespoons rum or brandy
4 ounces dark chocolate, broken into squares
2 tablespoons milk
2 cups heavy cream
2 tablespoons strong black coffee
16 ladyfingers
DECORATION
⅔ cup heavy cream
½ cup sliced almonds, toasted
½ ounce dark chocolate, melted

SERVES 8

1 Lightly grease a 5-cup loaf pan. Line with waxed paper or nonstick baking parchment. Using the almonds, water and sugar, make and grind the praline, as for Praline Ice Cream. Transfer the praline to a large mixing bowl and set aside.

2 Soak the raisins in half the rum or brandy for at least 1 hour. Melt the chocolate with the milk in a heatproof bowl over a pan of barely simmering water. Let cool.

3 Whip the heavy cream in a large mixing bowl until soft peaks form, then whisk in the chocolate. Fold in the praline and the soaked raisins, with any liquid.

4 Mix the coffee and the remaining rum or brandy in a shallow dish. Dip half the ladyfingers, one at a time, in the mixture, and arrange them in a layer on the bottom of the pan.

5 Cover with the chocolate mixture, then add another layer of dipped soaked ladyfingers. Cover the torte and freeze overnight.

6 Turn the frozen torte out onto a serving plate. Carefully remove the lining paper. Cover with the whipped cream, sprinkle the toasted almonds on top and drizzle on the melted chocolate. Serve in slices.

70

White Chocolate & Strawberry Torte

INGREDIENTS

4 ounces fine quality white chocolate, chopped
1/2 cup heavy cream
1/2 cup milk
1 tablespoon rum or vanilla extract
1/2 cup sweet butter, softened
3/4 cup superfine sugar
3 eggs
2 cups flour
1 teaspoon baking powder
pinch of salt
6 cups strawberries, sliced,
plus extra for decorating
3 cups whipping cream
2 tablespoons rum
WHITE CHOCOLATE MOUSSE FILLING
9 ounces fine quality white chocolate, chopped
1 1/2 cups whipping or heavy cream
2 tablespoons rum

SERVES 10

1 Preheat the oven to 350°F. Grease, and flour two 9-inch round cake pans, about 2 inches deep. Base-line the pans with nonstick parchment paper. Melt the chocolate in the cream in a double boiler over low heat, stirring until smooth. Stir in the milk and rum or vanilla extract. Set aside to cool.

2 Cream the butter and sugar until fluffy. Beat in the eggs one at a time. Sift together the flour, baking powder and salt. Stir into the egg mixture in batches, alternately with the melted chocolate, until just blended.

3 Divide the mixture between the pans. Bake for 20–25 minutes or until a cake tester inserted in the center of each cake layer comes out clean. Cool in the pans for 10 minutes. Turn out on to wire racks, peel off the parchment paper, and let cool.

4 Make the filling. Melt the chocolate with the cream in a saucepan over low heat, stirring frequently. Stir in the rum, and pour into a bowl. Refrigerate until just set, then whip the mixture lightly until it has a mousse-like consistency.

5 Slice each cake layer in half horizontally to make four layers. Spread a third of the mousse on top of one layer, and arrange a third of the strawberries over the mousse. Place another cake layer on top of the first, and cover with mousse and strawberries as before. Repeat this process once more, then top with the final cake layer.

6 Whip the cream with the rum. Spread about half the flavored cream over the top and sides of the cake. Use the remaining cream and strawberries to decorate the cake.

Luxury Mocha Mousse

INGREDIENTS

8 ounces good-quality semisweet chocolate, chopped
4 tablespoons espresso or strong coffee
2 tablespoons butter, cut into pieces
2 tablespoons brandy or rum
3 eggs, separated
pinch of salt
3 tablespoons superfine sugar
½ cup heavy or whipping cream
2 tablespoons Kahlua
chocolate-covered coffee beans, to garnish (optional)

SERVES 6

1 In a saucepan over medium heat, melt the chocolate in the coffee, stirring frequently until smooth. Remove from the heat and beat in the butter and brandy or rum.

2 In a small bowl, beat the egg yolks lightly, then whisk in the melted chocolate; the mixture will thicken. Set aside to cool. In a large bowl, beat the egg whites with an electric mixer. Add a pinch of salt and beat on medium speed until soft peaks form. Increase the speed and beat until stiff peaks form. Beat in the sugar, 1 tablespoon at a time, beating well after each addition until the egg whites are glossy and stiff.

3 Mix a large spoonful of whites into the chocolate mixture to lighten it, then fold the chocolate into the remaining whites. Spoon into 6 individual dishes or a large glass serving bowl and chill for at least 3–4 hours, until set, before serving.

4 In a medium bowl, beat the cream and Kahlua until soft peaks form. Spoon into an icing bag fitted with a medium star tip and pipe rosettes or shells on top of the mousse. Decorate with chocolate-covered coffee beans, if using.

Chocolate Cheesecake Pie

INGREDIENTS

1 1/2 cups cream cheese, softened
4 tablespoons heavy cream
1 cup sugar
1/2 cup cocoa powder
1/2 teaspoon ground cinnamon
3 eggs
BASE
1 1/2 cups graham cracker crumbs
8 amaretti cookies, crushed
(or extra graham cracker crumbs)
1/3 cup sweet butter, melted
DECORATION
whipped cream
chocolate curls

SERVES 8

75

1 Preheat the oven to 350°F. Make the base by mixing the crushed cookies with the melted butter. Press the mixture evenly over the bottom and sides of a 9-inch pie pan. Bake for 8 minutes, then let cool. Leave the oven on, and put a cookie sheet inside so that it heats up.

2 Beat the cheese and cream in a bowl with an electric mixer until smooth. Beat in the sugar, cocoa and cinnamon until blended. Then add the eggs, one at a time, beating for just long enough to combine. Pour the filling into the crumb shell, and bake on the hot cookie sheet for 25–30 minutes. The filling will sink as the cheesecake cools. Decorate with whipped cream and chocolate curls when cold.

Chocolate Fudge Torte

INGREDIENTS

8 ounces bittersweet chocolate, chopped
½ cup sweet butter, diced
⅔ cup water
1 cup sugar
2 teaspoons vanilla extract
2 eggs, separated
⅔ cup sour cream
2½ cups flour
2 teaspoons baking powder
1 teaspoon baking soda
pinch of cream of tartar
chocolate curls, raspberries and confectioner's
sugar, to decorate
CHOCOLATE FUDGE FILLING
1 pound bittersweet chocolate, chopped
1 cup sweet butter
5 tablespoons brandy
¾ cup seedless raspberry preserve
GANACHE
1 cup heavy cream
8 ounces bittersweet chocolate, chopped
2 tablespoons brandy

SERVES 18–20

1 Preheat the oven to 350°F. Base-line, and grease a 10-inch springform pan. Place the chocolate, sweet butter and water in a pan. Heat gently, until melted.

2 Pour into a large bowl, and beat in the sugar and vanilla extract. Let cool, then beat in the egg yolks. Fold in the sour cream. Sift the dry ingredients, then fold them into the mixture. Whisk the egg whites in a bowl until stiff, and gently fold in.

3 Pour the mixture into the pan. Bake for 45–50 minutes. Let cool for 10 minutes, then remove from the pan. Let cool completely on a wire rack.

4 Make the fudge filling. Gently melt the chocolate and butter with 4 tablespoons of brandy. Set aside to cool. Meanwhile, cut the cake into three layers. Heat the preserve with the remaining brandy, and spread over each cake layer. Let set.

5 Return the bottom layer to the pan, and spread with half the filling. Top with the middle cake layer. Spread over the remaining filling, add the top cake layer, and press down gently. Refrigerate overnight.

6 Make the ganache. Bring the cream to a boil, remove from the heat, and stir in the chocolate, then the brandy. Strain, then set aside for 5 minutes to thicken. Remove the cake from its pan. Pour the ganache over the top, and cover the sides. Pipe any remaining ganache around the base of the cake using a star-shape nozzle. When set, decorate with chocolate curls, raspberries and confectioner's sugar. Do not refrigerate the glazed cake.

Ice Creams & Sorbets

If you've never made your own ice cream, now is the time to try. It isn't difficult, just follow these easy recipes. Start with family favorites such as classic Vanilla and Chocolate Ice Cream, then move on to contemporary variations, such as Brown Bread Ice Cream, or serve a simple ice with a rich or fruity and colorful sauce. For a simple, easy-to-prepare dessert, choose a low-fat frozen treat and make a refreshing sorbet. Lime & Mango Sorbet in Lime Shells will make a stunning finale to any meal.

Vanilla Ice Cream

INGREDIENTS

1¼ cups heavy cream
1 vanilla bean or ½ teaspoon vanilla extract
2 eggs, lightly beaten
¼ cup sugar
blackberry sauce, to serve (optional)

SERVES 4

1 Pour the cream into a heavy saucepan. Add the vanilla bean, if using. Bring the mixture to just below the boiling point. Remove the vanilla bean.

2 Place the eggs and sugar in a heat-proof bowl. Set the bowl over a pan of barely simmering water and whisk until the mixture is pale and thick. Whisking vigor-  ously, pour in the cream in a steady stream. Continue to whisk the mixture just until it begins to thicken.

3 Whisk in the vanilla extract, if using. Cool, then spoon into a suitable container for freezing. Freeze until crystals form around the edges, whisk until smooth, then freeze again.

4 Repeat the process once or twice, then freeze the mixture until firm. Alternatively, use an ice cream maker, following the manufacturer's instructions. Let the ice cream soften slightly before serving in scoops, with a fruit sauce, if desired.

VARIATION
Make a less rich version of the ice cream by substituting buttermilk for three-quarters of the heavy cream, and using 2 tablespoons honey instead of the sugar.

Chocolate Ice Cream

INGREDIENTS

8 ounces semi-sweet chocolate, broken into squares
3 cups milk
1 vanilla bean
4 egg yolks
½ cup sugar

SERVES 4–6

1 Half fill a saucepan with water, let boil, then remove from heat. Place the chocolate in a heatproof bowl over the pan. Set aside until the chocolate has melted, stirring occasionally.

2 Pour the milk into a heavy saucepan. Add the vanilla bean. Keeping the heat fairly low, bring the mixture to just below the boiling point. Remove the vanilla bean.

3 Place the egg yolks in a large heatproof bowl and whisk in the sugar. Whisk in the hot milk, then add the melted chocolate. Place the bowl over a

pan of barely simmering water and stir until the chocolate custard thickens slightly. Let cool.

4 Spoon the mixture into a suitable container for freezing. Freeze until ice crystals form around the edges of the container, then process or beat the mixture

until smooth. Repeat the process once or twice, then freeze the mixture until firm. Alternatively, use an ice cream maker, following the manufacturer's instructions. Let the ice cream soften slightly before serving it in scoops.

81

Rhubarb & Orange Ice

INGREDIENTS

12 ounces pink rhubarb
grated zest and juice of 1 medium orange
2 tablespoons honey
1 teaspoon powdered gelatin
quartered orange slices, to decorate

SERVES 4

82

1 Trim the rhubarb and slice it into 1-inch lengths. If you have not been able to obtain pink (forced) rhubarb, and the stems are a bit stringy, peel them thinly before slicing.

2 Put the rhubarb into a saucepan and add half the orange zest and juice. Bring to the simmering point and cook over very low heat until the rhubarb is just tender. Stir in the honey.

3 Heat the remaining orange juice, then remove from heat. Stir in the gelatin until it has completely dissolved, then stir the liquid into the rhubarb, and add the remaining orange zest.

4 Transfer the mixture to a suitable container for freezing. Freeze until ice crystals form around the edges and the mixture is slushy.

5 Scrape the mixture into a bowl and beat until smooth. Return it to the freezer and freeze until firm. Let the ice soften slightly before serving it in scoops, decorated with quartered orange slices.

COOK'S TIP

Pink (forced) rhubarb is naturally quite sweet, but you may find it necessary to add a little more honey—or sugar—to the mixture.

Fresh Orange Granita

INGREDIENTS

---

4 large oranges
1 large lemon
¾ cup sugar
2 cups water
blanched pared strips of orange and lemon zest,
to decorate
amaretti cookies, to serve

SERVES 6

1 Thinly pare the zest from the oranges and the lemon, taking care to avoid the bitter white pith. Use a vegetable peeler for best results. Set a few pieces

aside for decoration. Cut the fruit into segments and squeeze the juice into a pitcher. Set aside.

2 Heat the sugar and water in a heavy saucepan, stirring over low heat until the sugar has dissolved. Bring the mixture to a boil, then boil without stirring for about 10 minutes until a syrup forms. Do not let the syrup to burn on the saucepan bottom.

3 Remove the syrup from the heat. Then add the orange and lemon zest and shake the pan. Cover and let the syrup cool. The zest will infuse the syrup.

4 Strain the sugar syrup into a shallow freezer container and add the fruit juice. Stir well to mix, then freeze, uncovered, for about 4 hours or until slushy.

5 Mix the ice with a fork. Then freeze until it sets hard —about 4 hours. To serve, let sit at room temperature for 10 minutes, then break up with a fork and pile into

long-stemmed glasses. Decorate with strips of zest and serve with amaretti cookies.

Hazelnut Ice Cream

INGREDIENTS

¾ cup hazelnuts
6 tablespoons sugar
2 cups milk
1 vanilla bean
4 egg yolks

SERVES 4–6

1 Spread the hazelnuts on a baking sheet. Place under a medium broiler for about 5 minutes, shaking the sheet often, until the nuts are toasted. Let them cool slightly, then rub off the outer skins with a clean dish towel. Chop very finely or grind in a food processor or nut mill, with 2 tablespoons of the sugar.

2 Pour the milk into a heavy saucepan. Add the vanilla bean and bring the mixture to just below the boiling point. Remove the vanilla bean.

3 Place the egg yolks in a heatproof bowl. Whisk in the remaining sugar, then the hot milk. Place the bowl over a pan of barely simmering water and stir in the ground hazelnuts. Stir until the custard thickens slightly, then let cool.

4 Spoon the mixture into a suitable container for freezing. Freeze until ice crystals form around the edges, then process or beat the mixture until smooth. Repeat the process twice, then freeze until the mixture is firm. Alternatively, use an ice cream maker, following the manufacturer's instructions. Let the ice cream soften slightly before serving it in scoops.

Brown Bread Ice Cream

INGREDIENTS

½ cup hazelnuts, toasted and ground (see
Hazelnut Ice Cream)
1½ cups fresh whole-wheat bread crumbs
⅓ cup brown sugar
3 egg whites
½ cup sugar
1¼ cups heavy cream
few drops of vanilla extract
fresh mint sprigs, to decorate
SAUCE
1½ cups black currants, thawed
if frozen
6 tablespoons sugar
1 tablespoon crème de cassis

SERVES 6

2 Whisk the egg whites in a greasefree bowl until stiff peaks form, then gradually whisk in the sugar until thick and glossy. Whip the cream to soft peaks; fold it into the meringue with the bread crumb mixture and vanilla extract. Spoon the mixture into a 5-cup loaf pan. Level the surface, then cover and freeze until firm.

3 Meanwhile, make the sauce. Put the black currants in a bowl with the sugar. Toss gently, cover and set aside for 30 minutes, then purée in a blender or food processor. Press through a nylon sieve into a bowl, stir in the crème de cassis and chill well. Serve the ice cream in slices, with the sauce. Decorate with the fresh mint sprigs.

I Spread out the ground hazelnuts and bread crumbs on a baking sheet. Sprinkle on the brown sugar. Broil the hazelnuts under medium heat until the mixture is crisp and browned. Let cool.

Turkish Delight Ice Cream

INGREDIENTS

1¼ cups milk
4 egg yolks
½ cup sugar
1 cup rose-flavored Turkish delight, chopped
2–3 tablespoons water
1 tablespoon rosewater
1¼ cups heavy cream
thin almond cookies, to serve (optional)

SERVES 6

88

1 Bring the milk to a boil in a large heavy pan. Whisk the egg yolks with the sugar in a heat-proof bowl. Then whisk in the hot milk.

2 Place the bowl over a pan of barely simmering water and stir until the custard thickens slightly. Remove from heat, cover the surface of the custard closely with waxed paper (to prevent the formation of a skin) and let cool.

3 Meanwhile, heat the Turkish delight and water in a small pan. When most of the mixture has melted, and only a few lumps remain, stir it into the cold custard, with the rosewater and cream.

4 Spoon the mixture into a suitable container for freezing. Freeze until ice crystals form around the edges, then transfer to a bowl and whisk the mixture well. Return to the freezer container. Repeat the process once or twice, then freeze until firm. Alternatively, use an ice cream maker, following the manufacturer's instructions. Let the ice cream soften slightly before serving it in small scoops with the thin almond cookies, if using.

COOK'S TIP
This ice cream will look extra special decorated with a sprinkling of pink rose petals, if you have any.

Coconut Ice Cream

INGREDIENTS

14-ounce can evaporated milk
14-ounce can condensed milk
14-ounce can coconut milk
1 teaspoon grated nutmeg
1 teaspoon almond extract
lemon balm sprigs, lime slices and shredded
coconut, to decorate

SERVES 8

1 Mix the evaporated milk, condensed milk and coconut milk in a large bowl that will fit in the freezer. Stir in the nutmeg and almond extract.

2 Freeze until ice crystals begin to form around the edges of the mixture, then remove from the freezer and whisk by hand or with a hand-held beater until the  mixture is fluffy and has almost doubled in bulk.

3 Transfer the mixture to a suitable container for freezing, cover and freeze until solid. Let the ice cream soften slightly before serving in scoops, decorated  with lemon balm sprigs, lime slices and the shredded coconut.

Kulfi

INGREDIENTS

3 14-fluid ounce cans evaporated milk
3 egg whites
2⅔ cups confectioners' sugar
1 teaspoon ground cardamom
1 tablespoon rosewater
1½ cups pistachios, chopped
¾ cup sliced almonds
½ cup golden raisins
3 tablespoons candied cherries, halved

SERVES 4–6

1 The process of heating evaporated milk in its can may prove to be dangerous. We prefer to pour the evaporated milk in a pan. Bring to a boil, lower the heat, cover and simmer for 20 minutes. Cool and refrigerate for 24 hours.

2 Whisk the egg whites in a greasefree bowl until stiff peaks form. Open the cans and pour the milk into a chilled bowl. Whisk until doubled in bulk, then fold in the egg whites and confectioners' sugar.

3 Gently fold in the ground cardamom, rosewater, nuts, golden raisins and cherries. Cover the bowl and freeze until ice crystals form around the edges, then mix well with a fork. Return to the freezer and freeze again until firm. Let the kulfi soften slightly before serving it in scoops.

Mint Ice Cream

INGREDIENTS

2½ cups light cream
1 vanilla bean or ½ teaspoon vanilla extract
8 egg yolks
6 tablespoons sugar
¼ cup finely chopped fresh mint
fresh mint sprigs, to decorate

SERVES 8

92

1 Pour the cream into a heavy saucepan. Add the vanilla bean, if using. Keeping the heat fairly low, bring the mixture to just below the boiling point. Remove the vanilla bean.

2 Place the egg yolks and sugar in a large mixing bowl. Beat until the mixture is pale and light, using a balloon whisk or an electric beater. Transfer to a pan.

3 Whisking vigorously, pour the hot cream into the saucepan in a steady stream. Continue to whisk until the mixture thickens slightly. Whisk in the vanilla extract, if using. Let cool.

4 Stir in the mint. Spoon the mixture into a suitable container for freezing. Freeze until ice crystals form around the edges, then beat the mixture until smooth.

5 Repeat the process once or twice, then freeze until firm. Alternatively, use an ice cream maker, following the manufacturer's instructions. Let the ice cream stand at room temperature for 15 minutes before serving, to soften slightly. This ice cream looks spectacular scooped into an ice bowl, decorated with the fresh mint sprigs.

Rocky Road Ice Cream

INGREDIENTS

4 ounces semi-sweet chocolate,
broken into squares
⅔ cup milk
1¼ cups heavy cream
1½ cups marshmallows, chopped if large
½ cup candied cherries, chopped
½ cup crumbled shortbread
2 tablespoons chopped walnuts

SERVES 6

94

2 Whip the cream in a bowl until it just holds its shape. Beat in the chocolate milk, then transfer the mixture to a suitable container for freezing. Freeze until ice crystals form around the edges. Alternatively, churn the mixture in an ice cream maker until it is thick and almost frozen.

3 Using a spatula, stir the marshmallows, chopped candied cherries, crumbled shortbread and walnuts into the frozen mixture. Freeze again until it is firm. Let the ice cream soften slightly before serving it in scoops or slices.

1 Melt the squares of chocolate in the milk in a large saucepan over low heat, stirring occasionally. Let the chocolate milk cool completely.

COOK'S TIP
Use kitchen scissors to chop the marshmallows, dipping
the blades in a pan of boiling water between snips.

Coffee Ice Cream with Caramelized Pecans

INGREDIENTS

1 ¼ cups milk
1 tablespoon dark brown sugar
1 tablespoon instant coffee granules
1 egg, plus 2 yolks
1 ¼ cups heavy cream
1 tablespoon sugar
CARAMELIZED PECANS
1 cup pecan halves
⅓ cup dark brown sugar
2 tablespoons water

SERVES 4–6

96

1 Heat the milk and 1 tablespoon brown sugar in a heavy saucepan, stirring until the sugar dissolves. Bring to a boil, remove from heat and stir in the instant coffee until dissolved.

2 Combine the egg and extra yolks in a heatproof bowl. Set the bowl over a saucepan of barely simmering water, and whisk until the eggs are pale and thick. Remove from heat.

3 Whisking vigorously, pour in the coffee-flavored milk in a steady stream. Replace over the water and stir until the custard thickens slightly. Let the mixture cool.

4 Whip the cream with the sugar until soft peaks form. Fold it into the coffee custard, then transfer the mixture to a suitable container for freezing. Freeze until ice crystals form around the edges, then beat the mixture until smooth. Repeat the process once or twice, then freeze until firm. Alternatively, use an ice cream maker, following the manufacturer's instructions.

5 Caramelize the pecans. Preheat the oven to 350°F. Spread the nuts in a single layer on a baking sheet. Bake for 10–15 minutes, checking frequently, until they are roasted.

6 Next, dissolve ⅓ cup brown sugar in the water over low heat, then bring to a boil. When the mixture bubbles and begins to turn golden, add the  roasted pecans. Cook for 1–2 minutes over medium heat, until the pecans are well coated.

7 Spread the pecans on a lightly oiled baking sheet and set aside until they have cooled. Let the ice cream soften slightly at room temperature before serving it in scoops, with the caramelized pecans.

Mixed Berry Frozen Yogurt

INGREDIENTS

5 cups mixed berries (such as raspberries, strawberries, black currants, red currants)
¾ cup red grape juice
1 tablespoon powdered gelatin
2 eggs, separated
1 cup plain yogurt

SERVES 6

1 Set half the fruit aside for the decoration. Purée the rest in a blender or food processor, then rub through a sieve into a bowl, to remove any seeds.

2 Heat the grape juice in a small pan until just below the boiling point. Remove from heat and sprinkle the gelatin on the surface. Stir the grape juice to dissolve the gelatin completely. Cool slightly.

3 Whisk the egg yolks, yogurt and dissolved gelatin into the fruit purée. Pour into a suitable container for freezing. Freeze until crystals form around the edges and the mixture is slushy.

4 Whisk the egg whites in a grease-free bowl until stiff peaks form. Transfer the half-frozen yogurt into a bowl and quickly fold in the egg whites.

5 Return the mixture to the freezer container and freeze until solid. Soften slightly before serving in scoops, with the reserved berries.

COOK'S TIP

Hull the fruit used for the purée, but leave the rest whole—attached to the stems—for the decoration.

Mango Sorbet with Mango Sauce

INGREDIENTS

2 14-ounce cans sliced mangoes, drained
½ teaspoon lemon juice
grated zest of 1 orange and 1 lemon
4 egg whites
¼ cup sugar
½ cup heavy cream
½ cup confectioners' sugar

SERVES 4–6

100

1 Purée the mangoes in a blender or food processor. Transfer half the purée into a large bowl, which will fit in the freezer. Stir in the lemon juice and citrus zest.  Reserve the remaining purée for the sauce.

2 Whisk the egg whites in a greasefree bowl until stiff peaks form, then gradually whisk in the sugar until thick and glossy. Fold into the mango purée and freeze until ice crystals form around the edges of the bowl.

3 Beat the mixture until it is smooth, then scrape into a freezer container and freeze until firm.

4 Make the mango sauce. Whip the heavy cream with the confectioners' sugar until soft peaks form, then fold in the reserved mango purée. Spoon into a serving bowl,  then cover the bowl and chill for 24 hours.

5 Let the sorbet soften for about 10 minutes before serving in scoops, topped with the sauce.

Watermelon Sorbet

INGREDIENTS

2¼-pound piece of watermelon
1 cup sugar
juice of 1 lemon
1½ cups water
2 egg whites
fresh mint leaves, to decorate

SERVES 6

1 Cut the watermelon into cubes, discarding the rind and any seeds. Mash a quarter of the cubes in a shallow bowl. Purée the remaining watermelon in a blender or food processor, in batches if necessary.

2 Mix the sugar, lemon juice and water in a saucepan. Stir over low heat until the sugar dissolves, then boil, without stirring, for 2 minutes. Transfer to a large bowl and stir in the watermelon purée and the mashed watermelon. Cool, then pour the mixture into a suitable container for freezing.

3 Freeze until ice crystals form around the edges of the mixture, then scrape it into a bowl and beat until smooth. Freeze the mixture as before, then beat and freeze again.

4 In a greasefree bowl, whisk the egg whites until they form soft peaks. Beat the frozen mixture again, then fold in the egg whites. Return the sorbet to the freezer container, freeze for 1 hour, then beat again and freeze until firm. Let the sorbet soften before serving in scoops, decorated with the fresh mint leaves.

101

Chocolate Sorbet with Red Berries

INGREDIENTS

2 cups water
3 tablespoons honey
½ cup sugar
¾ cup unsweetened cocoa powder
2 ounces semi-sweet chocolate,
broken into squares
3 cups red berries (such as raspberries,
strawberries, red currants), to serve

SERVES 6

102

2 Remove the saucepan from heat, add the chocolate, a few squares at a time, and stir until melted. Set the saucepan aside until the mixture has cooled.

3 For a really fine texture, churn the mixture in an ice cream maker until it has completely frozen. Alternatively, pour the mixture into a container suitable  for use in the freezer, freeze until slushy, then whisk until smooth and freeze again. Whisk for a second time before the mixture hardens completely.

4 Let the sorbet soften slightly at room temperature before serving in scoops or ovals, decorated with the berries.

1 Mix the water, honey and sugar in a large saucepan. Gradually add the cocoa powder, and stir continuously until the liquid is smooth. Cook gently over low  heat, stirring occasionally, until the sugar and cocoa have dissolved completely.

COOK'S TIP

To shape the sorbet into ovals, use two tablespoons. Scoop out the sorbet with one tablespoon, then use the other to smooth it off and transfer it to a plate.

Black Currant Sorbet

INGREDIENTS

1 ¼ pounds black currants
½ cup sugar
½ cup water
1 tablespoon egg white
fresh mint sprigs, to decorate

SERVES 4

1 Strip the black currants from their stems by pulling them through the tines of a fork. Mix the sugar and water in a saucepan. Stir over low heat until the sugar dissolves, then boil, without stirring, for 2 minutes.

2 Purée the black currants with the lemon juice in a blender or food processor. Add the sugar syrup and process briefly to mix. Press the mixture through a sieve set over a bowl to remove any seeds.

3 Pour the black currant purée into a nonmetallic container suitable for use in the freezer. Cover and freeze until ice crystals form around the edges and the mixture is slushy.

4 Scrape spoonfuls of sorbet into a blender or food processor. Process until smooth, then, with the motor running, add the egg white and process until well mixed.

5 Return the sorbet to the freezer container and freeze until almost firm. Process again. Serve immediately or return to the freezer until solid, in which case the sorbet should be allowed to soften slightly before serving. Serve in scoops, decorated with the fresh mint sprigs.

Lime & Mango Sorbet in Lime Shells

INGREDIENTS

4 large limes
1½ teaspoons powdered gelatin
1 ripe mango, peeled and chopped
2 egg whites
1 tablespoon sugar
pared lime zest strips, to decorate

SERVES 4

1 Slice the tops off the limes, and take a slim slice off the bottom of each so that they stand upright. Carefully scoop the flesh into a bowl, keeping the lime shells intact. Squeeze out all the juice from the lime flesh and put 3 tablespoons of it in a small heatproof bowl. Sprinkle the gelatin on top and set aside until spongy.

2 Purée the mango with the remaining lime juice (about 2 tablespoons) in a blender or food processor. Place the heatproof bowl over a small pan of hot water and stir until the gelatin has dissolved completely. Add it to the mango purée and process briefly to mix.

3 Whisk the egg whites in a grease-free bowl until they form soft peaks. Whisk in the sugar, then fold into the mango mixture. Spoon into the lime shells, mounding the mixture. Freeze any excess sorbet in ramekins.

4 Freeze the filled shells until firm, wrap them in plastic wrap and replace them in the freezer. Before serving, unwrap the limes and let the sorbet soften slightly. Decorate with the lime zest strips.

105

Specialties

Think of the heat of summer, and the ideal dessert that springs to mind is always something cool and refreshing. This connoisseur's collection of tried and tested specialty frozen desserts contains something for every taste, and all of the desserts are made in advance of the occasion with components that can be assembled quickly and easily at the last minute. For an ice cream extravaganza, serve glorious Black Forest Sundaes, and for a spectacular finale, choose a lush and colorful layered Cranberry Bombe decorated with your choice of colorful additions.

Coffee Granita

INGREDIENTS

½ cup sugar
2 cups water
1 cup very strong black coffee, cooled
cookies, to serve
DECORATION
1 cup heavy cream, whipped with
2 teaspoons confectioners' sugar

SERVES 4

108

2 Add the coffee to the sugar syrup in the saucepan and combine. Then pour the mixture into a shallow freezer tray and freeze for several hours until it is solid.

3 To remove from the freezer tray, plunge the bottom of the container into very hot water for a few seconds, then turn out the frozen coffee mixture and chop it into large chunks.

4 Place the frozen coffee chunks in a food processor and process until the ice breaks down to a mass of small crystals. Spoon into tall serving glasses and top each glass with a spoonful of the sweetened whipped cream.

1 Mix the sugar and water in a saucepan. Stir over low heat until the sugar dissolves, then boil, without stirring, for about 2 minutes. Remove from heat and let cool.

COOK'S TIP

If you do not wish to serve the granita immediately, pour the processed mixture back into the freezer tray and freeze until serving time. Thaw for a few minutes before serving, or process again.

Praline Ice Cream in Cookie Baskets

INGREDIENTS

½ cup blanched almonds
¼ cup water
¾ cup sugar
2 cups milk
6 egg yolks
1 cup heavy cream
8 cookie baskets, to serve

SERVES 6–8

110

2 Break the nut praline into small pieces. Grind in a food processor until fine. Then, in a large saucepan, bring the milk to just below the boiling point.

1 Brush a baking sheet lightly with oil. Mix the nuts, water and 5 tablespoons of the sugar in a saucepan. Stir over low heat until the sugar dissolves, then boil, without stirring, until the syrup is a medium caramel color and the nuts begin to pop. Carefully pour the nuts onto the baking sheet and set aside until cold.

3 Whisk the egg yolks and remaining sugar in a heatproof bowl until pale and thick. Whisk in the hot milk, then place the bowl over a pan of simmering water and stir until the mixture thickens. Remove the bowl from heat and stir in the heavy cream. Set aside to cool.

4 Stir the praline into the mixture, reserving 2 tablespoons for decoration. Churn in an ice cream maker until frozen. Alternatively, pour it into a freezer container, freeze until slushy, whisk until smooth, then freeze again. Whisk for a second time before the mixture hardens completely.

5 Let the ice cream soften before serving, in the baskets, sprinkled with the reserved praline.

Black Forest Sundae

INGREDIENTS

14-ounce can pitted black cherries in syrup
1 tablespoon cornstarch
3 tablespoons kirsch
⅔ cup whipping cream
1 tablespoon confectioners' sugar
2½ cups chocolate ice cream
4 ounces chocolate cake, cut in large pieces
vanilla ice cream, to serve
8 fresh cherries, to decorate

SERVES 4

1 Strain the cherry syrup into a large saucepan, then spoon 2 tablespoons of the syrup into a small bowl. Stir in the cornstarch until the mixture is smooth.

2 Bring the syrup in the pan to a boil. Stir in the cornstarch mixture, lower the heat and simmer briefly to thicken. Add the cherries, stir in the kirsch and spread the mixture out on a baking sheet to cool.

3 In a bowl, whip the cream with the confectioners' sugar until soft peaks form. Place a spoonful of the cherry mixture in each of four sundae glasses. Top with layers of chocolate ice cream, pieces of chocolate cake, whipped cream and more cherry mixture, until the glasses are almost full.

4 Finish off each sundae with a final piece of chocolate cake, two scoops of ice cream and a whirl of fresh whipped cream. Decorate each with 2 fresh cherries and serve immediately.

VARIATION

This particular sundae is based on Black Forest Cake, but you don't have to be tied to these ingredients. Invent your own combinations of fruit, ice cream, cake and cream.

Blackberry & Apple Romanoff

INGREDIENTS

4 apples
3 tablespoons sugar
1 cup whipping cream
1 teaspoon grated lemon zest
6 tablespoons plain yogurt
4–6 crisp meringues, roughly crumbled
1½ cups fresh or thawed frozen blackberries
whipped cream, blackberries and fresh
mint sprigs, to decorate

SERVES 6

114

2 Whip the cream with the remaining sugar in a large mixing bowl. Fold in the grated lemon zest and yogurt, then stir in the mashed apples and the meringues.

3 Gently stir in the blackberries, then transfer all of the mixture to the pudding basin. Cover the mold with plastic wrap and freeze for 1–3 hours, until the mixture is firm.

4 Turn out onto a chilled plate, lift off the plastic wrap and pipe whipped cream around the base. Decorate with the blackberries and fresh mint sprigs.

1 Line a 4-cup pudding mold with plastic wrap. Peel and core the apples, then slice them into a heavy frying pan. Add 2 tablespoons of the sugar. Cook the mixture for 2–3 minutes or until the apples soften. Mash them with a fork and set the frying pan aside to cool.

Cranberry Bombe

INGREDIENTS

SORBET CENTER
2 cups fresh or frozen cranberries, thawed if
frozen, plus extra to decorate
⅔ cup orange juice
finely grated zest of ½ orange
½ teaspoons allspice
⅓ cup sugar
OUTER LAYER
1 batch Vanilla Ice Cream
2 tablespoons chopped angelica
2 tablespoons mixed citrus peel
1 tablespoon sliced almonds, toasted

SERVES 6

1 Line a 5-cup pudding mold with plastic wrap. Make the sorbet center. Put the cranberries, orange juice, zest and allspice in a saucepan. Cook

gently until the cranberries are soft. Stir in the sugar, then purée the mixture in a food processor until almost smooth, but with some texture. Set the saucepan aside to cool.

2 Allow the Vanilla Ice Cream to soften slightly, then transfer it to a bowl and stir in the chopped angelica, mixed citrus peel and sliced almonds.

3 Pack the mixture into the prepared pudding mold and use the back of a dessert spoon to hollow out the center. Cover and freeze until firm.

4 Fill the hollow in the ice cream with the cranberry mixture. Freeze again until firm. When ready to serve, invert the bombe on a chilled plate and

lift off the plastic wrap. Let the bombe soften slightly at room temperature before serving it in slices, decorated with fresh cranberries.

COOK'S TIP

This luxurious frozen dessert tastes great on hot summer evenings, but it also makes a wonderful alternative to Christmas Pudding. It is easy to make, popular with children and requires absolutely no attention on the day!

Frozen Apple & Blackberry Terrine

INGREDIENTS

1 pound apples
1 ¼ cups apple juice
1 tablespoon honey
1 teaspoon vanilla extract
2 cups fresh or thawed frozen blackberries
1 tablespoon powdered gelatin
2 egg whites
fresh apple slices and blackberries, to decorate

SERVES 6

2 Purée the apples, with the honey and vanilla extract, in a blender or food processor. Spoon half the apple purée into a bowl and set it aside. Add half the blackberries to the remaining apple purée and process until smooth. Press the blackberry and apple purée through a sieve to remove the seeds.

3 Then, pour the remaining apple juice into the clean pan and bring to just below the boiling point. Sprinkle the gelatin over and stir until completely dissolved. Stir half the gelatin into the plain apple purée and half into the blackberry and apple purée. Let both purées cool until they are on the verge of setting.

4 Whisk the egg whites until almost stiff, then fold them into the plain apple purée. Spoon half the mixture into a separate bowl. Stir in the remaining whole blackberries. Then transfer the mixture to a 7½-cup loaf pan, packing it down firmly. Top with the blackberry purée, spreading it level, then the remaining apple purée. Freeze the mixture until firm. Let the terrine soften slightly before serving it in slices, decorated with the fresh apple slices and the blackberries.

1 Peel, core and chop the apples. Place them in a saucepan with half the apple juice. Bring to a boil, then cover and simmer the apples gently until they are tender.

Fried Wontons & Ice Cream

INGREDIENTS

oil, for deep-frying
12 wonton wrappers
8 scoops of your favorite ice cream (or
4 scoops each of two varieties)

SERVES 4

120

1 Heat the oil in a deep-fryer or large saucepan to 350°F or until a cube of dried bread browns in 30–45 seconds.

2 Add a few wonton wrappers at a time, so that they do not crowd the pan too much. Fry for 1–2 minutes on each side, until the wrappers are crisp and light golden brown. Lift out and drain on paper towels.

3 To serve, place one wonton on each plate. Top with a scoop of ice cream, then add a second wonton and a second scoop of ice cream. Finish with a final wonton. Serve immediately.

COOK'S TIP

Mix and match the scoops of ice cream to contrast the colors but take care to choose complementary flavors. Try coffee with hazelnut, Turkish delight with vanilla or chocolate with mint.

Café Glacé

INGREDIENTS

2½ cups water
2–3 tablespoons instant coffee granules
1 tablespoon sugar
2½ cups milk
6 ice cubes
12 scoops of vanilla ice cream
6 chocolate kisses, to decorate
12 crisp cookies, to serve

SERVES 6

1 Bring ½ cup of the water to a boil, pour into a small bowl and stir in the coffee granules. Stir in the sugar until dissolved. Let cool, then chill for about 2 hours.

2 Mix the milk and remaining water in a large pitcher. Add the chilled coffee mixture and mix well. Divide the mixture among six brandy snifters or cocktail glasses, filling them three-quarters full.

3 Add an ice cube and 2 scoops of vanilla ice cream to each glass. Decorate with the chocolate kisses and serve with the cookies.

Mint & Chocolate Cooler

INGREDIENTS

¼ cup hot chocolate mix
1¾ cups chilled milk
⅔ cup plain yogurt
½ teaspoon peppermint extract
4 scoops of chocolate ice cream
mint leaves and chocolate shapes, to decorate

SERVES 4

122

2 Pour the liquid into a large mixing bowl or large pitcher and whisk in the remaining milk. Then, add the plain yogurt and the peppermint extract.

3 Pour the mixture into four tall glasses and top each with a scoop of chocolate ice cream. Decorate each of the glasses with the fresh mint leaves and assorted chocolate shapes. Serve immediately.

I Place the hot chocolate mix in a small saucepan and stir in about ½ cup of chilled milk. Gently heat the liquid, stirring constantly, until almost boiling, then remove the saucepan from heat and let the liquid cool.

COOK'S TIP
Unsweetened cocoa powder can be used instead of hot chocolate mix, if preferred, but remember that cocoa can be quite bitter: you may need to add sugar to taste.

Blushing Piña Colada

INGREDIENTS

1 banana
1 thick slice of pineapple
5 tablespoons pineapple juice
1 scoop strawberry ice cream or sorbet
1½ tablespoons coconut milk
1 small scoop finely crushed ice (see Cook's Tip)
2 tablespoons grenadine
stemmed maraschino cherries, to decorate

SERVES 2

1 Peel the banana and chop it roughly. Cut two small wedges from the pineapple and set aside for the decoration. Then peel and chop the remaining pine-

apple and add it to the blender with the banana and pineapple juice. Process to a smooth purée.

2 Add the strawberry ice cream or sorbet to the blender. Pour in the coconut milk and add the scoop of finely crushed ice. Process until smooth.

3 Then, divide the drink between two large, well-chilled glasses. Trickle the grenadine syrup on top of the piña colada; it will filter through the drink to give a blush pink effect.

4 Slit the reserved pineapple wedges, and slip one onto the rim of each glass. Then add a maraschino cherry in the same way. Serve the blushing piña colada with drinking straws.

COOK'S TIP

Never try to crush ice in a blender;
it will ruin the blades. Put the ice cubes in a
strong plastic bag and crush them finely with
a rolling pin before adding to the blender.

124

Ice Cream Strawberry Shortcake

INGREDIENTS

*3 6-inch ready-made sponge cake cases or
shortcakes
5 cups vanilla or strawberry ice cream,
softened until spreadable
5 cups hulled strawberries, halved if large
whipped cream, to serve (optional)*

SERVES 4

126

1 If you are using sponge cake cases, trim off the raised edges with a sharp serrated knife. The sponge trimmings can be saved and used to make individual treats.

2 Using two-thirds of the ice cream and hulled strawberries, sandwich the sponge cake cases or shortcakes together.

3 Spoon the remaining ice cream on top, and crown with the remaining strawberries. Serve the shortcake immediately, with whipped cream, if desired.

COOK'S TIP

There is no neat way of cutting this delicious dessert. It will look glorious until you actually start to serve it, and that's what really matters.

Index